Send a Baby

Luke 1:5–25; 57–64

(The Birth of John the Baptist)

by Mary Manz Simon
Illustrated by Dennis Jones

SAINT LOUIS

Books by Mary Manz Simon from Concordia Publishing House

Hear Me Read Level 1 Series
What Next?
Drip Drop
Jibber Jabber
Hide the Baby
Toot! Toot!
Bing!
Whoops!
Send a Baby
A Silent Night
Follow That Star
Row the Boat
Rumble Rumble
Who Will Help?
Sit Down
Come to Jesus
Too Tall Too Small
Hurry Hurry!
Where Is Jesus?

Hear Me Read Big Books Series
What Next?
Drip Drop
Send a Baby

Follow That Star
Sit Down
Come to Jesus
Too Tall Too Small
Where Is Jesus?

Hear Me Read Level 2 Series
The No-Go King
Hurray for the Lord's Army!
The Hide-and-Seek Prince
Daniel and the Tattletales
The First Christmas
Through the Roof
A Walk on the Waves
Thank You Jesus

Little Visits® Series
Little Visits on the Go
Little Visits for Toddlers
Little Visits with Jesus
Little Visits Every Day

Stop! It's Christmas
God's Children Pray
My First Diary

Copyright © 1992 Concordia Publishing House
3558 S. Jefferson Avenue, St. Louis, MO 63118-3968
Manufactured in the United States of America

Library of Congress Cataloging-in-Publication Data

Simon, Mary Manz, 1948–
    Send a baby : Luke 1:5-26, 57-64, the birth of John the Baptist / by
Mary Manz Simon ; illustrated by Dennis Jones.
        (Hear me read Bible stories)
    "A complete story in only 25 words."
    Summary, a simple retelling of the events surrounding the birth of
John the Baptist.
    ISBN 0-570-04706-4
    1. John, the Baptist, Saint—Juvenile literature. 2. Bible stories,
English—N.T. Luke. [1. John the Baptist, Saint. 2. Bible Stories—N.T.] I.
Jones, Dennis, ill. II. Title. III. Series: Simon, Mary Manz, 1948– Hear
me read Bible stories.
BS2456.s55 1992
226.4'09505—dc20
                                                                91-7381
                                                                CIP
                                                                AC

04 05 06 07 08 09 10 11 12   09 08 07 06 05 04 03 02 01 00

Name
_____

Date
_____

Presented by

_____

To the Adult:

Early readers need two kinds of reading. They need to be read to, and they need to do their own reading. The Hear Me Read Bible Stories series helps you to encourage your child with both kinds.

For example, your child might read this book as you sit together. Listen attentively. Assist gently, if needed. Encourage, be patient, and be very positive about your child's efforts.

Then perhaps you'd like to share the selected Bible story in an easy-to-understand translation or paraphrase.

Using both types of reading gives your child a chance to develop new skills and pride in reading. You share and support your child's excitement.

As a mother and a teacher, I anticipate the joy your child will feel in saying, "Hear me read Bible stories!"

Mary Manz Simon

For Hank
Psalm 104:33

"I want a baby,"
said Elizabeth.
"I want a baby,"
said Zechariah.

Elizabeth and Zechariah
prayed to God.
Elizabeth and Zechariah
prayed to God for a baby.

"I want a baby,"

said Elizabeth.

"I want a baby,"
said Zechariah.

Elizabeth and Zechariah
prayed to God.
Elizabeth and Zechariah
prayed to God for a baby.

Will God send a baby?

Elizabeth and Zechariah

prayed and prayed.

Will God send a baby?

God sent an angel.

God's angel said,

"God will send a baby.

God will send baby John."

Zechariah said, "Oh?"

God's angel said,

"You do not believe God.

You will not talk."

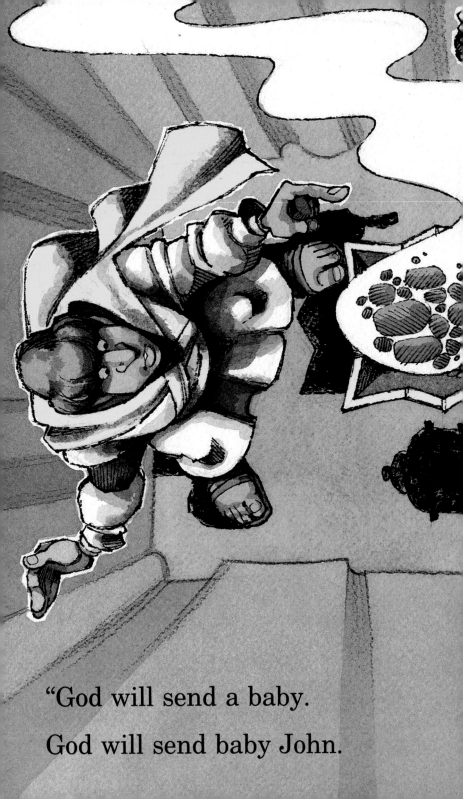

"God will send a baby.

God will send baby John.

Then you will talk."

God sent a baby.

God sent baby John.

Zechariah talked.

Zechariah said,

"I believe God.

I do believe God.

"God sent a baby.

God sent baby John."

About the Author

Mary Manz Simon holds a doctoral degree in education with a specialty in early childhood education. She has taught at levels from preschool through postgraduate. Dr. Simon is the best-selling author of more than 40 children's books, including *Little Visits with Jesus*. She and her husband, the Reverend Henry A. Simon, are the parents of three children.